GRAMERCY GREAT MASTERS

Sandro Botticelli

Gramercy Books
New York • Avenel

Acknowledgments

The publishers would like to thank the museums for reproduction permission and in particular the **BRIDGEMAN ART LIBRARY** for their help in supplying the illustrations for the book.

Alte Pinakotek, Munich: Pietà.
Anicabegg-Stockar, Zurich: St. Thomas Aquinas.
Royal Chapel, Grenada: The Agony in the Garden.
Galleria degli Uffizi, Florence: Infant Christ Embracing the Madonna (Madonna of the Loggia); Madonna and Child in a Glory of Seraphim; Madonna and Child (Madonna of the Rosebush); The Finding of the Body of Holofernes; The Return of Judith; Portrait of a Man with a Medal of Cosimo the Elder; The Adoration of the Magi; Primavera; The Annunciation; Pallas and the Centaur; The Birth of Venus; Madonna of the Magnificat; Madonna of the Pomegranate; The Annunciation; Madonna and Child Enthroned with Four Angels and Six Saints; The Coronation of the Madonna and Four Saints; Sacred Scene (from the predella of the St. Mark Altarpiece); Sacred Scene (from the predella of the St. Mark Altarpiece); The Calumny of Apelles.
Isabella Stewart Gardner Museum, Boston: Madonna and Child with an Angel Bearing Grain and Grapes (Madonna of the Eucharist).
National Gallery, London: The Adoration of the Magi; Portrait of a Young Man; Venus and Mars; The Mystic Nativity.
Ognissanti, Florence: St. Augustine in his Cell.
Pinacoteca di Brera, Milan: Madonna Under a Baldachin.
Prado, Madrid: The Story of Nastagio degli Onesti (First Episode); The Story of Nastagio degli Onesti (Second Episode); The Story of Nastagio degli Onesti (Third Episode).
Private collections: Dante Alighieri; The Story of Nastagio degli Onesti (Fourth Episode).
Pushkin Museum, Moscow: The Archangel Gabriel.

Published by Gramercy Books
a division of Random House Value Publishing, Inc.
40 Engelhard Avenue
Avenel, New Jersey 07001

Printed and bound in Italy

ISBN 0-517-18217-3

10 9 8 7 6 5 4 3 2

Sandro Botticelli
HIS LIFE AND WORKS

It was unusual for Sandro Botticelli to sign a painting. But despite this, his genius can be easily recognized in the many works he painted throughout his career. From *The Birth of Venus* to *Primavera*, from the frescoes in the Sistine Chapel to *The Mystic Nativity*—all these famous paintings confirm Botticelli's sure hand, his brilliance as a linear technician, his authority with color and form. Models seem to float in the air, fantastical landscapes echoing their lightness.

In a Botticelli painting, subject and background are flat, painted in pale, cool colors. There is no natural perspective, yet the painting is full of life. The grace of line, the expression in the faces, and the mystical themes set Botticelli apart from other Renaissance masters. His paintings evoke that immediate rush of feeling that here, at this moment, we are in the exhilarating, transporting presence of greatness.

The most striking elements in Botticelli's work are his larger-than-life allegorical figures. Walter Pater, a nineteenth-century English authority on the Italian Renaissance, described Sandro Botticelli's figures as "comely, and in a certain sense like angels, but with a sense of displacement or loss about them . . . the wistfulness of exiles . . . which runs through all his varied work with a sentiment of ineffable melancholy."

But there is more to Botticelli's work than his ability to create emotive figures and evocative lines. His paintings also reflect the changes in the way people of his day were thinking and living their lives.

A Shift in Art, Science, and Thought

The Early Renaissance had just begun when Botticelli became interested in art. People were looking back to the past, to classical Greece and Rome for inspiration in philosophy, science, and art.

Artists in the Middle Ages used classic lines and shapes to create sculpture and paintings, but the final result had to be religious—and serious. No "pagan" mythology was permitted in the soaring Gothic churches or the somber, musky, candlelit chapels. Venus always turned into a Madonna. Hercules became Samson. Plato, Aristotle, or Socrates would be recreated as one of the apostles. Europa captured by the bull emerged as Christ redeeming a soul.

With the advent of the Renaissance in the early fifteenth century, however, the prevailing viewpoints began to change, especially in the courts of the powerful Medicis in Florence. More important than the mayor, wealthy beyond imagination, the Medicis—Cosmo and Pietro, Lorenzo the Magnificent and Guiliano—were also at the forefront of avant-garde thought. They commissioned new artists; they welcomed scientists and philosophers to their court—especially those who expounded the Neo-Platonic philosophy of the Early Renaissance.

The Neo-Platonists and Botticelli

The Neo-Platonists rejected the medieval belief in an orderly and rigid universe. Instead, they believed that all life in the universe was linked to God through a spirit that was constantly in movement, continuously ascending and descending from the earth to heaven. Religious stories from the Bible, mythology from Greece, and symbols of Love, Beauty, and Fortitude were all part of this circuit. They were all one. Venus and the Madonna, for example, were the same, both depictions of divine beauty and divine love. Any spiritual representation, be it a myth or a passage from the Bible, could be portrayed for religious worship on church walls and chapel altars.

Botticelli embraced the Neo-Platonic movement. Neo-Platonic thought enabled him to combine the religious and the mythical, to explore religious thought as well as classical symbols. It enabled Botticelli to recreate the magnificent myths with their rites of spring, their love of beauty, their powerful evocations of adventure

10

and revelation. In this new world, Botticelli could be an important force in Early Renaissance art.

These were the times in which Botticelli lived, in which he flourished, and in which he later retired from public life and attention. It was a world changing, full of excitement and hope—and possibilities.

But as popular as Botticelli was with his public, Giorgio Vasari, the first chronicler of Renaissance artists, did not approve of him. In *Lives of the Most Eminent Painters, Sculptors, and Architects*, Vasari made reference to Botticelli's "ungovernable spirit" that could only end in wretchedness. Vasari frequently mentioned Botticelli's ties to the great families of Florence, the Medicis, the Vespuccis, and the Puccis. He wrote that Botticelli was considered a great master at forty years of age, only to throw it all away to concentrate on illustrating Dante's *Inferno* in 1500. As Vasari wrote: "Being a man of inquiring mind, he completed and printed a commentary on a part of Dante, illustrating the *Inferno*. He wasted a great deal of time on this, neglecting his work and thoroughly disrupting his life."

Indeed, drawn by an innate mysticism, by the intellectual symbolism and humanistic poetry of Dante's work, Botticelli did eventually leave the world of allegorical painting, church frescoes, and commissions from powerful Florentine families. By the early sixteenth century his work was considered unfashionable and was quite forgotten, virtually ignored until his rediscovery as a master painter almost four hundred years later.

BOTTICELLI: A MASTER IS BORN

There were no mandatory birth certificates in the Middle Ages; records have disintegrated to dust. But Sandro Botticelli is believed to have been born in 1445 in the Santa Maria Novella quarter of Florence. His earliest biographical record comes from his father, the tanner Mariano di Vanni Filipepi. In 1458 he had apparently filed a complaint to the Florence Registry about his thirteen-year-old son, Sandro, that the boy was "unhealthy" and "reading."

Not only did this official complaint enable historians to calculate Sandro's birth date, but it provided a clue to the painter's personality, already formed at the age of thirteen. He was frail, possibly melancholy, and he had a passion for independent intellectual pursuits, which was obviously not shared by his father. Nor were

*Portrait of a
Young Woman*
(detail)

his more aesthetic predilections shared with his brothers. Sandro inherited his nickname from his elder brother, Giovanni, who had first been called "botticelli" by a teasing co-worker. Apparently, Giovanni had a large, barrel-shaped torso, and in Italian, a "botticella" means small barrel or cask. Or perhaps Sandro got his name from another brother, Antonio, who was a gilder by trade. "Battigello" was a fifteenth-century name for a goldsmith. And it is known that Mariano, despairing of his son's future, had apprenticed Sandro to Antonio's workshop.

Unfortunately, goldsmithing was not the right calling for the frail, dreamy Botticelli, who had difficulty concentrating. But working in a gilding shop proved serendipitous. Artists, artisans, and painters came through the shop all the time. Botticelli became acquainted with some painters and, through them, found his true vocation: painting.

When Botticelli confessed to his father his desire to be a painter at any cost, Mariano, "knowing the force of his son's inclinations," acquiesced, and apprenticed his young son to Fra Filippo Lippi, the Early Renaissance master artist.

An Apprentice's Life

Botticelli was older than the other boys in Fra Filippo Lippi's workshop. In the fifteenth century most young aspiring artists had begun their apprenticeship by the time they were twelve. Botticelli was sixteen, but he was as determined as he was talented.

Botticelli was fortunate in his choice of masters. Fra Filippo was an idealist painter. One of the last devotional painters, he painted from the spiritual heart, unlike Raphael and da Vinci who were among the young naturalistic painters who believed in a scientifically based realism and painted what they saw.

In Fra Filippo's studio the idealistic, dreamy Botticelli was allowed to flourish. He learned the techniques of Masaccio, the first great Italian Renaissance painter whose classically balanced frescoes, with their skillfully rendered models in light and shadow, influenced many artists of the day.

Botticelli also learned the masterful techniques of Fra Filippo himself. His influence is obvious in Botticelli's earliest works, all of them on religious subjects, including *Madonna of the Loggia*, *Guidi Madonna*, *Madonna and Child*, and *Madonna of the Rose Garden*. But even in these first paintings, the characteristic heavy lines of Fra Filippo's hand have given way to Botticelli's clean, slender lines, to his unique airy compositions where lines pursue one another, intertwine, then break way again in slow-moving rhythms.

Botticelli not only learned composition and insight in Fra Lippi's workshop, he also perfected his painting technique. He almost always painted in egg tempera and became a master of this medium. He rarely painted on canvas, preferring to work on panels of wood, especially walnut. To prepare the wood's surface he used powdered flake white and Chinese white mixed with carpenter's glue. He would apply this mixture in thin layers, sometimes as many as seven or eight, to create a smooth, workable surface. Using a stylus, Botticelli would then etch in his composition, filling in his lines with color, which he would also apply in several layers. He used casein tempera for a final glaze.

Botticelli was becoming a masterful painter in his own right. He was beginning to paint with confidence and expertise. Combined with the exhilarating environment of Florence, at the height of its artistic, economic, and political splendor, it would appear that there was no stopping him.

WORKING WITH VERROCCHIO

In 1467, Fra Filippo Lippi received an important commission from the city of Spoleto. He was to decorate their cathedral. Botticelli stayed behind in Florence: it was time for him to go his separate way.

When Fra Lippi left for Spoleto, Botticelli went to work for the painters Andrea Verrocchio and the Pollaiuolo brothers, Piero and Antonio. All three painters belonged to the naturalistic school that was growing in Renaissance Italy. They believed in the importance of scientific experimentation and research to create realistic art. From them Botticelli learned about space, foreshortening, and perspective, and came to understand how the human body moved. These were the last technical lessons Botticelli needed to become a great master, in complete control of his art.

Some critics believe Botticelli was already working on his own in 1467, that he learned to paint more realistically from observing Verrocchio's work, which was extremely popular and in great evi-

14

dence in Florence at the time and not from actually working with Verrocchio himself. But the truth remains that *The Baptism of Christ*, attributed to Verrocchio and his apprentice, the young Leonardo da Vinci, has unmistakable traces of Botticelli's hand. Perhaps Botticelli was a partner in the workshop, or a senior artist. If so, he probably supervised the pictorial work, while the older and better known Verrocchio (or, perhaps, the Pollaiuolo brothers) prepared actual cartoons for the paintings and directed the gilding and sculpture. But whether Botticelli worked for a more experienced artist or not, he continued to learn his craft and hone his vision. He was ready for his own commissions.

ON HIS OWN

In 1470, Botticelli officially became an independent painter in Florence. He opened a workshop and received his first commission. It was one panel in a series illustrating the seven *Virtues* for the Tribunal of the Arts della Mercanzia, the Merchant's Guild, of Florence. The Pollaiuoli had received the actual commission and they gave *Fortitude* to Botticelli to do on his own.

Fortitude was Botticelli's first documented independent work. The original commission for the *Virtues* cycle came from the court of the powerful Medicis. It was significant that Botticelli was contributing to the series. It meant that he embraced the Neo-Platonic philosophy expounded by the Medicis. They refused to patronize Verrocchio or da Vinci because their work was too scientific, too realistic for their taste. They wanted someone who could understand the all-encompassing, classical nature of the spirit, its continuous cycle between heaven and earth, between mythology and religiosity, between the biblical and mythical symbols.

In Botticelli the Medicis found their artistic representative. *Fortitude* was a complete success. The melancholy beauty of Botticelli's earlier Madonnas, with their bowed heads and pensive facial expressions, was still here, but in *Fortitude* it had taken the form of an idle, dreaming spirit, a mythical symbol whose vigorless grasp on a mace is the antithesis of might. The panel's gilded decorative elements show that Botticelli's training as a goldsmith had not been not wasted.

Fortitude assured Botticelli a place in Florence's artistic world. In 1472, he joined the Artists' Company of St. Luke, which further

*The Temptation
of Moses*
(from the Sistine Chapel)
(detail)

guaranteed him new commissions. (His brother, Antonio, even joined the company a short time later in the hopes of receiving gilding work.)

Then Lorenzo de Medici—the legendary Lorenzo the Magnificent—commissioned Botticelli to paint *St. Sebastian* for the central nave of the Church of Santa Maria Maggiore. Here was proof not only of Botticelli's merit as an artist, but of his ability to respond to the wishes of Florence's most important and influential family.

Botticelli worked on *St. Sebastian* for one year, from 1473 to 1474. The painting is a magnificent example of his early style. Its symmetry and cool elegance show Verrocchio's influence. The saint's position puts all his weight on one foot, accentuating the inclination of his head and giving him an ephemeral quality. The expression on his face betrays no sign of pain. Indeed, the pain seems to have been transformed into sorrow, pervaded by the vague air of melancholy Botticelli had begun to perfect.

In 1474, Botticelli received proof that his reputation had spread beyond the borders of his city. He was asked to create frescoes for the Camposanto cemetery in Pisa. But although the officials in Pisa were impressed with Botticelli's work in Florence, they were not completely confident of his abilities and asked him to submit a sample painting of the *Assumption*. If they liked what he did, he would be free to begin the frescoes. Although the records in Pisa show that Botticelli ordered a good quantity of ultramarine for painting, the *Assumption* was never finished and the half-completed work was destroyed in 1583.

Whether the rejection came from Botticelli or his employers will never be known, but he never did the frescoes. He returned home more determined than ever to become a great artist who would never have to succumb to a "test" again.

MORE COMMISSIONS

Back in Florence, Botticelli's fame continued to grow. The debacle of the Pisa frescoes faded by the time he was commissioned to do a tournament banner for Giuliano de Medici in January 1475. Giuliano, Lorenzo's younger brother, was also a hero among the citizens of Florence, who wrote poems about his bravery as well as his appearance.

Primavera
(detail)

As was the custom of the day, men who were to joust in a tournament required a standard-bearer as introduction. The bearer held a banner that symbolized the bravery and fame of the jouster who would soon enter the arena. For Botticelli to paint such a banner was indeed a privilege.

Unfortunately, all traces of the banner have disappeared. But Vasari, that great Renaissance diarist, describes it as similar to Botticelli's *Pallas and the Centaur*, which was painted in 1480, most probably as a wall decoration. It is a classical myth Botticelli favored: Athena, the great goddess of wisdom, takes the name Pallas as her own when her sister Pallas is killed. Pallas Athena, forever after, represents wisdom and protection. The story brings wisdom, selflessness, and heroism into play.

In Botticelli's painting, the allegory represents a celebration of the political power of the Medicis. The three interlocked rings scattered on Pallas Athena's gown are a Medici symbol. She is crowned by the olive branch of peace, a peace due to Lorenzo the Magnificent's wisdom in foiling a conspiracy in Naples in 1479. In her hand she grasps the hair of a cringing centaur, who represents the defeat of discord.

Pallas and the Centaur not only displayed Botticelli's mastery of paint and composition, it also showed how all-encompassing the classical revivalism of Neo-Platonism had become intellectually, artistically, and in every facet of life in the early Renaissance. Classical mores, allegories, and structure had not only become a supreme ideal, they had also become fashionable.

Botticelli flourished in this climate. He painted many classical allegories. In addition to *Pallas and the Centaur*, there is *Venus and Mars*, also painted around 1480. In this painting Mars is asleep, being watched over by Venus, the incarnation of Humanity, of Divine Love, who dissolves strife and warfare and puts peace in the hearts of all. The embodiment of the intellectual and spiritual ideals of Neo-Platonic Florence, she was a form Botticelli created again and again in his art.

This panel was probably painted for another powerful Florentine family, the Vespuccis. In the right-hand corner there is a cluster of wasps, the Vespucci family emblem. (Vespucci, in Italian, means "little wasps.") The allegory of Sleep being watched over by a protective Venus would be a fitting decoration for a wedding chest, and the painting might have been commissioned for a

The Birth of Venus
(detail)

wedding, since there are four baby satyrs between the two reclining gods. They are toying with Mars' weapons and introduce a playful element into the concept of "wedded bliss."

In 1480, the Vespucci family also commissioned Botticelli to execute the *St. Augustine* fresco for the Church of the Ognissanti. Botticelli created an intellectual allegory. The saint, in his spartan cell, is surrounded by intellectual symbols, including parchment papers and ancient manuscripts. His expression is otherworldly; he is lost in philosophical speculation, intent on the investigation of elevated and difficult matters. He seems detached from his surroundings. The schematic drawing is washed with colors in the same range of soft hues. The outlines of the composition are penetrating and sharply balanced.

This combination of penetrating, harmonious lines and a subdued color range appears in a series of portraits Botticelli did during this same prolific period (1474-1480). They include the earlier *Portrait of a Young Man*, which some critics see as an attempt to follow the more somber Flemish examples, the later *Portrait of a Young Man with a Red Beret* and, painted in the clean-cut linear, style of artist Andrea del Castagno, *Portrait of Giuliano de Medici*, which was done after his friend Giuliano died. Botticelli painted a dove on a twig and a half-closed door—both of which are symbols of death.

Young Man with a Medal is considered the best of these portraits. It is yet another tribute to the great Medicis. The model is believed to be the metaphysical philosopher Giovanni Pico della Mirandola. He holds the gilded stucco medal of Cosimo de Medici, the first member of the dynasty.

Like other artists, in many of his paintings Botticelli used the Epiphany theme, which was popular in Florence at this time. The procession of kings gave artists the opportunity to portray—and glorify—well-known citizens and their families. A member of the Medici might be humbly bowing at the Magi. Someone from the Vespucci family could bear gifts. Indeed, Botticelli understood how well suited the subject was to the sensibilities of the new bourgeois families and painted several versions of *The Adoration of the Magi*.

Botticelli's first *Adoration of the Magi* was commissioned in 1476 for the Palazzo della Signoria. Unfortunately, it was destroyed when the palace was redecorated. His second *Adoration of the Magi* is one of his most famous paintings and it now hangs in the Uffizi Palace. It was commissioned around 1478 by a Florentine merchant, Giovanni di Zanobi del Lami, for the altar of the Church of St. Maria Novella. This Magi is a tribute to the Medicis. Among the kings are Cosimo, Peiro, and Giovanni Medici, as well as Peiro's sons, Lorenzo the Magnificent and Giuliano. The artist himself is here too, portrayed as the young man in the yellow robe.

Lorenzo the Magnificent was so impressed with Botticelli's *Adoration* that he soon commissioned him to paint what would later be considered one of his greatest masterpieces.

PRIMAVERA

Created between 1477 and 1478, *Primavera* is the embodiment of Botticelli's love of classical myth, of the adventures and morals of pagan lore. Because both *Primavera* and the later *Birth of Venus* complement each other in composition and spirit, Vasari believed they were conceived as part of a cycle.

Whether or not this is true, both paintings stand alone as masterpieces. In *Primavera*, the rarified atmosphere and the elegant features perfectly evoke the pagan allegory of the rites of spring. Indeed, as Flora, an ethereal nymph, passes across the panel in her floral-decorated gown, the field bursts into flower as though by magic. The real world has been subtly interpreted through lines that take on almost musical values.

Primavera testifies to Botticelli's continued rejection of the burgeoning Renaissance desire to investigate the laws of nature, of creating formal works in which science and art are one. Instead, in *Primavera*, he looks at the beauty of the lost and idealized ancient world of myth and magic, creating a work of lyrical poetry.

The magic is inherent in the painting's theme. On the right, Zephyr is pursuing Chloris as she changes into Flora, the herald of spring. Cupid and Venus, Divine Love and Beauty, fill the central part of the work, while, to the left, the figures of Graces and Mercury, symbols of reason, dance. Some critics believe that the painting was created to immortalize Simonetta Cattaneo Vespucci, the woman who died of consumption at a young age and was loved by Giuliano de Medici beyond all reason. In *Primavera*, she lives again as Venus, reborn in the Elysian fields.

22

The Annunciation
(detail)

Primavera was a landmark work of art, not only for the cultivated Florentines, but for Botticelli as a maturing artist. The viewer is urged to go beyond the simple representational allegory, beyond the words of such ancient poets as Ovid and Apelius, who wrote about Venus. Instead, the flowing lines, the mysticism that embraces the composition, and the movement of color all force the viewer to examine the pure, spiritual value of Beauty beyond the surface lore. The painting seems to say that Beauty is the image and symbol of Truth—a Truth that is not immediate but is the fruit of long, patient, and devotional spiritual meditation.

At last, by 1480, with *Primavera* and other works of art, Botticelli, the son of a tanner, had achieved the acclaim he must have only dreamed about. Here he was, a member of Lorenzo the Magnificent's court, surrounded by exquisite costumes, dining at sumptuous night-long banquets, conversing with some of the world's greatest scientists, philosophers, musicians, and artists.

But more acclaim was yet to come.

THE SISTINE CHAPEL

In 1481, Pope Sixtus IV bestowed a great honor on Botticelli. Along with several other renowned artists, including Cosimo Rosselli, Domenico Ghirlandaio, and Pietro Perugino, he was summoned to Rome to paint the frescoes for the walls of the newly built Sistine Chapel. The Pope was pleased with Botticelli's rendering of *The Temptation of Moses*, *The Temptation of Christ*, and *The Punishment of Korah, Dathan, and Abiram* and paid the artist more money than the other collaborators.

Botticelli immediately squandered the money while in Rome. Despite his financial solvency, he found Rome a difficult place with its petty jealousies and subterfuge. He was more at ease painting a single episode than the sweeping narrative of the fresco. This commission was a great challenge for him.

But the frescoes themselves belie the artist's inner turmoil. They are pure Botticelli; they illuminate his genius. Even within the confines of the strict, episodic narrative, his characteristic rhythmic linework is evident in the faces of the daughters of Jethro in *The Temptation of Moses* episode, in the young firewood carrier in *The Temptation of Christ*, in other young women's faces. When restoration of the Sistine Chapel began in 1984, another Botticelli

24

*The Calumny
of Apelles*
(detail)

was revealed, one in which much gold leaf was used in the decoration.

In 1484, Botticelli returned to Florence.

THE HEIGHT OF SUCCESS

Botticelli was pleased to return to Florence, where he could concentrate on the singular subjects, the one-at-a-time episodes he was most comfortable creating. He began with a series of small paintings in a tondo format. These sacred paintings were used for private worship. The classic round shape imposed its own particular rhythm and structure on a painting, regardless of artistic style or subject.

In the tondo *Madonna of the Magnificat* (1485), Botticelli's lines are all directed toward the arch formed by the angels' arms. The angels hold the Virgin Mary's shining crown above her head, illuminating and glorifying her with rays of gold. The interpretation of the lyrical subject is characteristically unusual. It is a study of lyrical, rhythmic composition. Botticelli depicts the Virgin herself writing the music, the Magnificat, in a book held open for her by angels. He blends classical Neo-Platonic symbols into his religious tondo; the pomegranate, a symbol of Persephone, goddess of the Underworld, is held by both the Virgin and the Child in her lap. And, in a provocative use of form, Botticelli deliberately distorted the Madonna's wrist, creating a spatial illusion of a convex surface.

Madonna of the Pomegranate (1487) was inspired by the earlier *Magnificat* tondo. But here the Virgin is sadly thoughtful. She, the angels, and the child all have a melancholy air. The pomegranate symbol at the center of the work makes the already dreamlike atmosphere even more melancholy and mysterious. The tondo's rhythm and spirit are mirrored and reinforced by the curves of the Child's body and by the bowed heads of the angels surrounding the Madonna and Child.

In addition to the tondi, Botticelli was also busy painting the St. Barnabas Altarpiece. Here, earthly figures representing Passion in the foreground contrast with the ideal, serene vision of the Madonna and Child and her attending angels above. Botticelli uses harsh, bright colors to differentiate the figures, creating a vivid impression of separateness between the objective, natural world and an idealized, subjective one.

26

The Mystic Nativity
(detail)

THE BIRTH OF VENUS

While Botticelli worked on his tondi and his panels, he was also working on his masterpiece, *The Birth of Venus*, which he painted between 1485 and 1488. Here is a Venus reminiscent of *Primavera*, but more mature, more allegorical, more spiritual than "pagan." Here, Venus the goddess, born of the sea, is gently pushed to the shore by a shower of roses, which, as described in Ovid's *Metamorphoses*, represent Spring. Zephyr, who represents ideal love, is the god of the wind and gently blows the roses in Venus' direction. His blue cape is a heavenly color. Venus herself represents Divine Truth, Beauty, and Spiritual Motivation. Her long flowing hair is the color of gold, the color of divine revelation and truth. Chastity, one of the Graces, waits patiently for Venus. She wears a white robe and holds a mantle of red, an earthy, mortal color, to place over Venus as she comes to rest on shore. This painting, steeped in symbolism and allegory, unites Christianity and classicalism. "Pagan" birth and baptism are joined. Philosophy and religion can be one, an all-encompassing Divine look at the universe.

But *The Birth of Venus* is not just a tapestry of symbolic mystery. It is also a tour de force of composition and technique. Despite the realistic, detailed rendering of the landscape, strewn with leaves and flowers, the marvelous, idyllic, and timeless fable of *The Birth of Venus* remains magical. Here, the ethereal contemplation of Beauty is intertwined with exacting elements of line and color. Once again, Botticelli has subtly interpreted the real world through musical, lyrical lines that move in and out of Venus' flowing hair, the diaphanous, almost veil-like garments, the billowing mantle, the pale, unfamiliar sky. As Venus stands, a static, chaste, and bashful statue, the world around her moves and flows, ebbs and recedes.

With *The Birth of Venus*, Botticelli reached a new pinnacle of success. He continued to paint tondi, showcasing the Madonna. He also painted a dramatic *Annunciation*, with lines so masterful that the angel's wings seem to quiver, and a profoundly sorrowful *Lamentation*. But transition was in the air and his technique, his style, and his philosophical bent would irrevocably change.

THE LATER YEARS

By 1491, Botticelli was an artistic figure of power and acclaim. He was a member of almost all the artistic committees in Florence. In that year, he was in charge of the mosaic decoration for the St. Zenobius Chapel in Florence Cathedral. Although the work was never completed, he continued to be active in cathedral politics and joined the jury for the cathedral façade. But after 1492, a profound change began to occur in Botticelli's style and attitude.

He came under the influence of Savonarola, a religious leader who was beginning to create a stir throughout Florence. A Dominican priest, Savonarola preached in the streets and in the chapels, in a high-pitched, passionate voice that drove the Florentine citizens to near hysteria. By 1490, he was at the peak of his power. He believed in a more puritanical religion, a spiritual life devoid of "pagan" lore. Savonarola denounced realism. To him, the only true spiritual realism was Christianity.

Botticelli, whose lifelong melancholia spoke of unfulfilled conflicts, whose art displayed an ambiguity between his need for religiosity and his desire for physical beauty, found the answers he craved in Savonarola's philosophy. He became a passionate follower and his paintings changed. Lines were harsher, themes more anguished. Gone were the rites of spring and the classic Virtues. Figures of antiquity were no longer spiritual in their own right. They had to adhere to rigid moral and religious codes. Here, if not historically correct, was the religious essence of biblical tribulations, the symbols of martyrs, transgression, and spiritual salvation. This new attitude is exemplified in *The Calumny of Apelles,* which Botticelli painted in 1495.

Inspired by a description of an ancient Greek painting by Apelles, this unusually small panel depicts the lavish halls of Midas. The king is surrounded by Virtues and Sins. Fully draped, Suspicion and Ignorance whisper in his ears while Truth, an isolated figure, is nude and reminiscent of a Botticelli Venus. She points to heaven while a draped Penitence turns to look at her. Fraud and Deceit adjust her jewels and her hair. Calumny is dragging a youth by the hair toward the throne. Envy, a horrible, repellent figure, and Deceit stand nearby, ready to present Calumny to the King. The walls are lined with statues and sculptural friezes depicting human suffering.

Pietà
(detail)

The almost unreal luminosity of the sky, a uniform light blue, creates a flat, otherworldly background for the surreal scene, which has been executed with a vehemence. Gone are the serene, gentle lines of other Botticelli masterpieces. The lines are stronger, closer, almost angry in their passion, which corresponds to Savonarola's teachings, his puritanical spirituality and rejection of the natural, real world.

But no painting exemplifies Botticelli's new style more than *The Mystic Nativity*, painted in 1500. When Botticelli painted this panel, he had suffered much loss. His friend Lorenzo the Magnificent had died and Lorenzo's son had been banished from Florence. Worse, Savonarola, in a martyr's death, had been burnt in the Piazza della Signoria as an enemy of the state, and France was threatening the peace in every town, hamlet, and state in Italy.

The Mystic Nativity is not a traditional rendition of the subject; it is much more mystical and poetic. The small composition is balanced, if unorthodox. The Nativity in the center is isolated from the rest of the painting. On its left, spectators, including an angel, wear the olive branches of peace in their hair. On the right, another angel leads three shepherds to the manger. At the top, in a curving, round, flat-painted sky, angels dangle crowns and carry olive branches, the same olive branches of peace worn by the spectators. In the foreground, in front of the manger, men embrace angels while jeering devils peer at them from the jagged rocks.

Along the top of the painting is the famous signature of Botticelli, the only one he ever penned. It is part of an epitaph written in Greek. It reads: "I, Sandro, painted this picture at the end of the year 1500 in the troubles of Italy, in the half-time after the time that was prophesied in the 11th of John and the second woe of the Apocalypse when the Devil was loosened upon the earth for three years and a half. Afterward he shall be put in chains according to the twelfth woe, and we shall see him trodden underfoot as in this picture."

This trodden defeat is not depicted in *The Mystic Nativity*, but the meaning is clear. The Apocalypse is drawing near, as is Satan's downfall. With his defeat, the angels will celebrate in heaven and humankind will be free from evil. This was a message from Savonarola's teachings: the rebirth of the church and of humanity will occur with the defeat of the Antichrist.

THE END DRAWS NEAR

Botticelli's austere spirituality increased as the sixteenth century progressed. He withdrew from the artistic community in Florence and dedicated himself to a lifelong ambition: illustrating Dante's *Divine Comedy* on twenty-four parchment sheets. He had initially done the drawings for the engraved illustrations in 1481. Throughout the years he often returned to them, spending his spare time on his Neo-Platonic interpretations of the great classic. The drawings are extraordinary. Botticelli's exuberant lines enliven the angels' garments, the expressions on the characters' faces, the flowers and myrtle gardens of Eden.

But the more Botticelli concentrated on Dante, the less the world concentrated on him. Florentine citizens had found new artists, new masters, to revere, including Leonardo, Raphael, and Michelangelo. Naturalism, a realistic culmination of art and science, became the philosophy of the day. The High Renaissance had entered its glorious, harmonious, and awesome center stage.

Botticelli's mythical pagans and severe, moralistic religiosity were outmoded. They did not belong in this brave, new world. Although he did sit on the 1503 commission to decide where Michelangelo's *David* would be showcased, Botticelli, for the most part, kept out of sight. Finally, crippled and forgotten, he died on May 17, 1510. He was buried in the Church of the Ognissanti, in Florence.

But in his magnificent and timeless paintings, Botticelli still lives as much a mystery as his art. His figures are frozen, impervious, and undecipherable allegories. They can demonstrate the gallant adventures of the young Medici princes with the same brilliance as the greatest mysteries of the natural and spiritual universe. For Botticelli, a composition was only the framework for a hint, a suggestion, of an unknown and otherworldly truth, a framework hinted at through his enigmatic figures and their souls.

The true meanings behind Botticelli's paintings will never be known, just as the true passions of the times in which he lived will forever remain a mystery. The world has only what Botticelli chose to show and what history has reclaimed as its own: a great master in the great mystery called art.

Infant Christ Embracing the Madonna (Madonna of the Loggia)

Madonna and Child in a Glory of Seraphim

Madonna and Child (Madonna of the Rosebush)

Madonna and Child with an Angel Bearing Grain and Grapes (Madonna of the Eucharist)

The Adoration of the Magi (detail)

The Adoration of the Magi

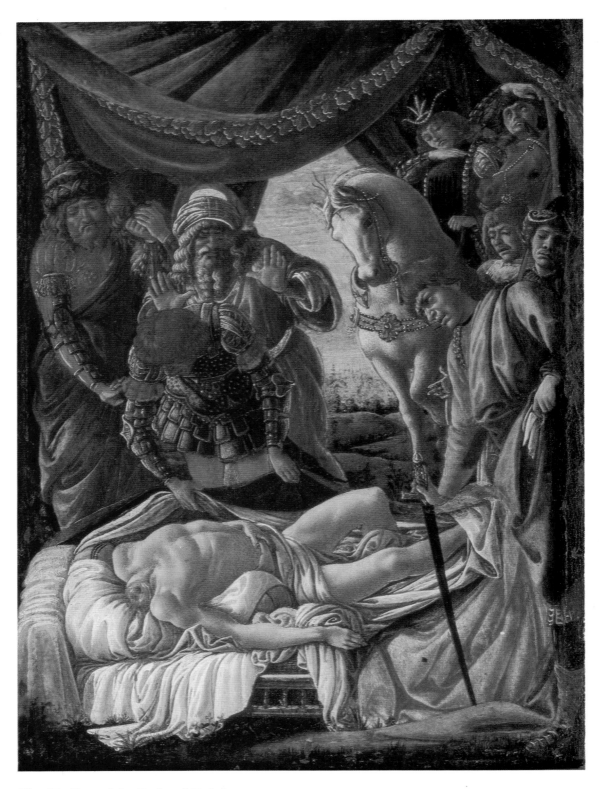

The Finding of the Body of Holofernes

The Return of Judith

Portrait of a Man with a Medal of Cosimo the Elder

St. Augustine in His Cell

The Adoration of the Magi

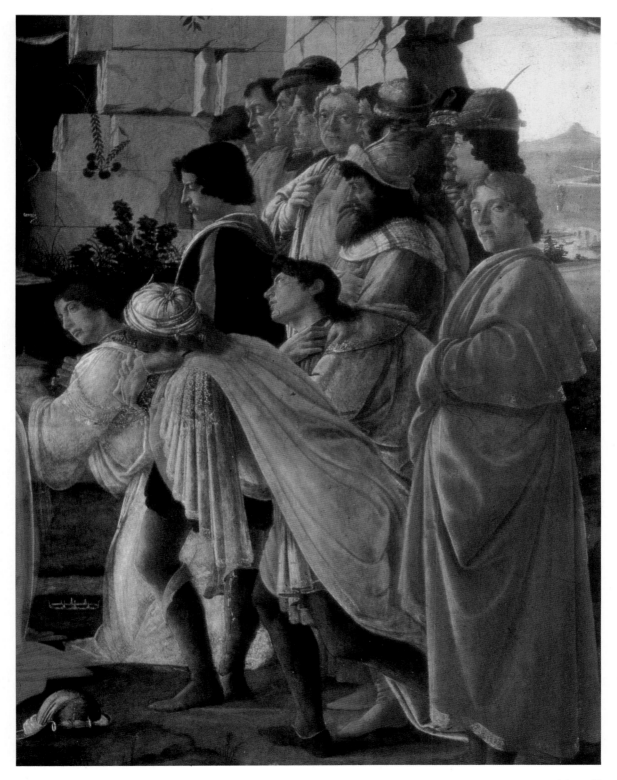

The Adoration of the Magi (detail)

Primavera

Primavera (detail)

Primavera (detail)

The Annunciation

Pallas and the Centaur

St. Thomas Aquinas

The Birth of Venus

The Birth of Venus (detail)

The Birth of Venus (detail)

Dante Alighieri

Portrait of a Young Man

Venus and Mars

The Story of Nastagio degli Onesti (First Episode)

The Story of Nastagio degli Onesti (Second Episode)

The Story of Nastagio degli Onesti (Third Episode)

The Story of Nastagio degli Onesti (Fourth Episode)

Madonna of the Magnificat

Madonna of the Magnificat (detail)

Madonna of the Pomegranate

Madonna of the Pomegranate (detail)

Madonna of the Pomegranate (detail)

Madonna and Child Enthroned with Four Angels and Six Saints

The Coronation of the Madonna and Four Saints

Sacred Scene (from the predella of the St. Mark Altarpiece)

Sacred Scene (from the predella of the St. Mark Altarpiece)

The Archangel Gabriel

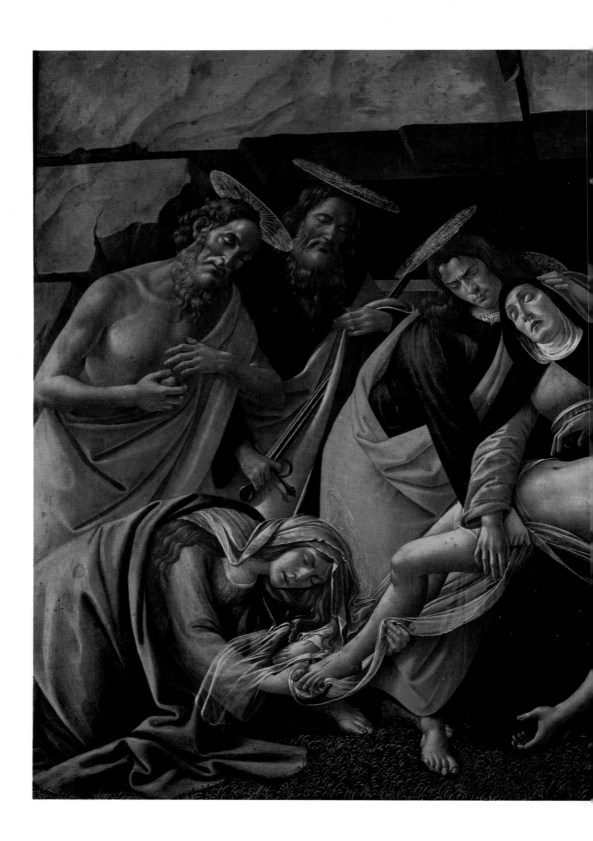

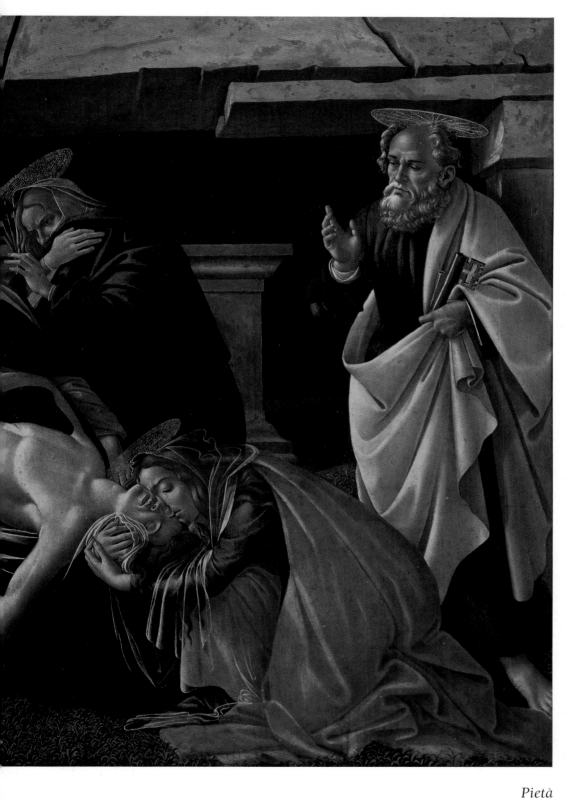

Pietà

Pietà (detail)

Pietà (detail)

The Annunciation

Madonna Under a Baldachin

The Calumny of Apelles

The Calumny of Apelles (detail)

The Calumny of Apelles (detail)

St. Augustine in His Cell

The Agony in the Garden

The Mystic Nativity

Stampa Grafiche Editoriali Padane Cremona